CLARISSE;

OR,

THE MERCHANT'S DAUGHTER.

A DRAMA

In Three Acts

BY

EDWARD STIRLING, ESQ.

Author of " Nicholas Nickleby." " Grace Darling." " Martin Chuzzlewit." " Blue Jackets." &c.

AS PERFORMED AT THE

THEATRE ROYAL, ADELPHI.

CORRECTLY PRINTED FROM THE PROMPTER'S COPY, WITH THE CAST OF CHARACTERS, COSTUME, SCENIC ARRANGEMENT, SIDES OF ENTRANCE AND EXIT, AND RELATIVE POSITIONS OF THE DRAMATIS PERSONÆ.

SPLENDIDLY ILLUSTRATED WITH AN ENGRAVING, BY MR. CLAYTON, TAKEN DURING THE REPRESENTATION OF THE PIECE.

LONDON:

PUBLISHED AT THE NATIONAL ACTING DRAMA OFFICE, 19, SUFFOLK-STREET, PALL-MALL EAST; TO BE HAD OF STRANGE, PATERNOSTER-ROW; WISEHEART, SUFFOLK-STREET, DUB-LIN; AND ALL RESPECTABLE BOOKSELLERS.

No. 121. Price 1s.

WEBSTER'S
ACTING NATIONAL DRAMA,

UNDER THE AUSPICES OF THE DRAMATIC AUTHORS' SOCIETY.

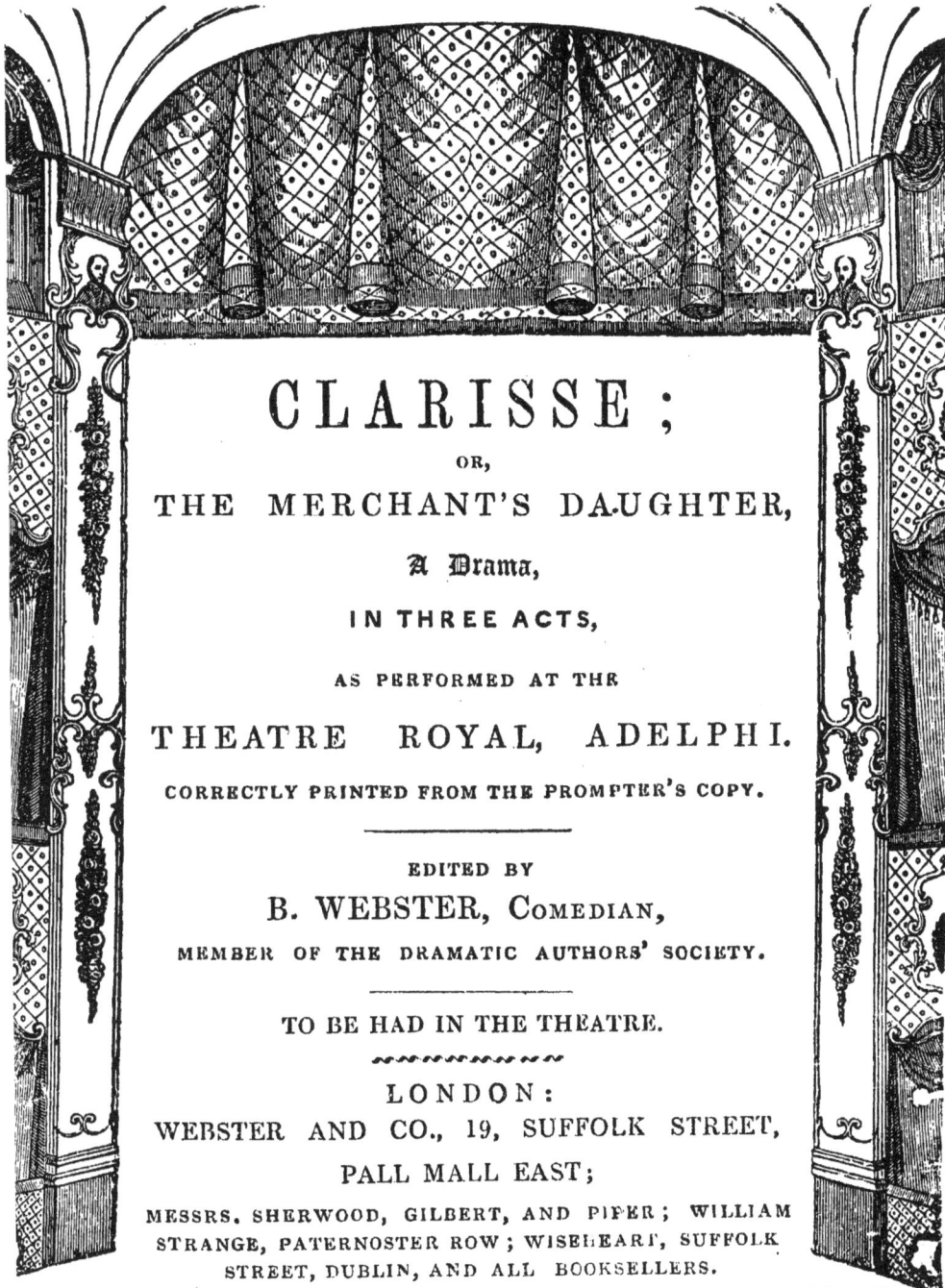

CLARISSE;

OR,

THE MERCHANT'S DAUGHTER,

A Drama,

IN THREE ACTS,

AS PERFORMED AT THE

THEATRE ROYAL, ADELPHI.

CORRECTLY PRINTED FROM THE PROMPTER'S COPY.

EDITED BY

B. WEBSTER, Comedian,

MEMBER OF THE DRAMATIC AUTHORS' SOCIETY.

TO BE HAD IN THE THEATRE.

LONDON:
WEBSTER AND CO., 19, SUFFOLK STREET,
PALL MALL EAST;

MESSRS. SHERWOOD, GILBERT, AND PIPER; WILLIAM
STRANGE, PATERNOSTER ROW; WISEHEART, SUFFOLK
STREET, DUBLIN, AND ALL BOOKSELLERS.

W. S. JOHNSON, "NASSAU STEAM PRESS," 60, ST. MARTIN'S LANE.

Dramatis Personæ and Costume.

First performed, Monday, September 1, 1845.

LA ROCHE. (*A Marchand de Bois, or wood merchant.*) Long brown coat, faced with black velvet, red and blue striped vest, blue trousers. (*Second dress.*) Blue dress coat, white vest, modern hat . . . - . . . . } MR. O. SMITH.

ROBERT. (*His foreman.*) Lavender striped vest, drab trousers, blue striped shirt. (*Second dress.*) Long brown coat, broad brimmed hat } MR. CHAS. PERKINS.

ARMAND. (*His clerk.*) Modern suit . . . . . MR. WORRELL.

MARTIAL. (*A gentleman at large.*) Blue coat, white vest, white cord French trousers, modern hat. (*Second dress.*) Green paletôt, red vest, checked trousers, French cap. (*Third dress.*) Green blouse, high black boots, French cap. (A strip to first dress.) . . . . . } MR. WEBSTER.

JOHN CABOT. (*His English tiger.*) Green frock coat, red cuffs and collar, red and white striped vest, white cord breeches, top boots, black hat, and silver band. (*Second dress.*) Ragged suit, as thief. (*Third dress.*) Long brown coat, chintz vest, red striped trousers, black cap, large peak, with false nose attached. (*Fourth dress.*) A strip or change, drab blouse, leather gaiters, French cap. (*Fifth dress.*) Green body coat, buff vest, black breeches, silk hose, shoes and buckles. opera hat . . . . } MR. MUNYARD.

BARBILLON. (*An equatic adventurer illustrating the purest water system.*) Ragged mixed cloth jacket, oil skin trousers, French cap. (*Second dress.*) Blue coat trimmed with white binding and scarlet tassels, scarlet vest, and pantaloons trimmed with white, black boots, cocked hat, tri-coloured feather. (*Third dress.*) Green coat, blue striped trousers, and vest, large white hat . . . . } MR. WRIGHT.

MONSIEUR JOSEPH. (*A banker.*) Morning dress . . . . } MR. FREEBORN

GALON. (*A specimen of a man above his work.*) Brown coat, grey striped trousers, blue striped shirt, black hat, crown hanging down. (*Second dress.*) Brown coat, red and white striped vest, small white hat . . . . } MR. PAUL BEDFORD.

NOTARY. Suit of black . . . .

MARTIN. Light blue coat, red chintz vest, grey striped trousers, French cap . . . . . . } MR. CULLENFORD.

PIPOD.
LOUCHON.
SLICK.
{ (*Adept appropriators of superabundant cash.*) As thieves, various coloured striped dresses, changing to full dress, with opera hat . . } MR. J. SANDERS.
MR. C. J. SMITH.
MR. MITCHENSON.

COMMISSAIRE OF POLICE. Blue coat, white facing, red cuffs and collar, white trousers and gaiters, cocked hat, tri-coloured cockade . . . . } MR. WAYE.

CLARISSE. Fawn-coloured silk dress. (*Second dress.*) White satin and orange flower wreath . . . . } MADAME CELESTE.

MILANIE. Modern Grisette's dress . . .   MISS WOOLGAR.

MADAME DONTEL. Modern dress . .   MRS. LAWS.

AGATHA. Modern French peasant's dress MISS REYNOLDS.

Chorus and Ballet Gentlemen.

1st. Act as workmen.—2nd Act in holiday clothes.

Time of representation, two hours and twenty minutes.

EXPLANATION OF THE STAGE DIRECTIONS.

L, means first entrance, left. R, first entrance, right. S.E.L. second entrance, left. S.E.R. second entrance, right. U.E.L. upper entrance, left. U.E.R. upper entrance, right. C. centre. L.C. left centre. R.C. right centre. T.E.L. third entrance, left. T.E.R. third entrance, right. Observing, you are supposed to face the audience.

ACT I.

SCENE I.—*A timber yard, arched entrance in flat leading to the canal.* R. *A counting house with the long roof, practicable window and door. A house, door, and window; door practicable,* L. *Platforms leading to the piles of wood. A dog kennel* R. *and a wall running from the arch enclosing the yard. When the curtain rises* MAD. DONTEL *is discovered at a table knitting.* L. ARMAND *is seated in the counting house, at a desk, writing.* GALON *and* MARTIN *at work. Several* WORKMEN *employed carrying logs up the platform, others bringing them from the quay through the archway,* MUSIC.

Mad. D. (calls.) Clarisse, Clarisse, my love! This is an extraordinary event; not in the wood yard before breakfast. She that is so active—such a woman of business in her father's absence. Oh, it's love! love makes all our heads spin round like a tee-to-tum.

Arm. (to the Men.) Pile the wood in front of the door lads.

Mar. It is doing, sir.

> [ARMAND *leaves the counting house and meets* CLARISSE, *who enters.* C.

Arm. Is not the work done quickly, Ma'amselle Clarisse?

Cla. Yes, my father must be pleased by this activity, on his return.

Gal. (comes from C. *Sits* R. *to fan himself with his hat,)* I'm done up.

Mar. Finish your work, man.

Gal. It's nothing but work here; one had better be a nigger at once.

Mar. Hold your tongue, dont you see Ma'mselle Clarisse.

Gal. I do, and respect her. She does'nt treat workmen like slaves; but as for her father, Laroche, he's no man, he sucks all the sugar and gives us nothing but the cane—a regular scrub.

Cla. Silence! I will not suffer any person to abuse my father in my presence.

Mad. D. It is your own fault, you are too kind to these men, above all, to Robert.

Gal. He's a nice man, Mons. Robert, very, with his orders and his fines.

Cla. You ought to obey him as your foreman. He is an active and faithful servant, and has lived with us fifteen years.

Mad. D. I would'nt have kept him fifteen days; he is sulky, and always quarrelling with the men.

Cla. With those only who neglect their duty. You are too severe.

Mad. D. And you too indulgent. (ARMAND *talks to* CLARISSE.) Talking again! That young fellow thinks to win the daughter and get all the old man's money.

[CLARISSE *goes into counting house* S. E. R. *and examines book.*

Arm. How beautiful she is! If I dared confess my passion for her. *(sighs).* But I am too poor. I must wait till I'm ——

Cla. (reading). 245, just right. *(leaves counting house).* Your accounts are correct, Monsieur.

Gal. I'm parched up. A cup of wine, or I shall die—come.

Mar. If Robert see you there'll be a dispute.

Gal. Who cares for *his* disputes. Aint we all alike. Come boys, a cup of wine.

ROBERT *enters from the arch* C. *and arrests their steps.*

Rob. When your work's done. Neither you or any man in the yard shall waste his master's time while I have control here.

Gal. Only a taste, Mr. Robert, a gentle taste?

Rob. You spend too much of your time in the wine shops. We want no idle drunken workmen. You would feel it hard if your master robbed you of a portion of your wages; then, by what right do you rob him of his time?

Mar. Robert's right. No one ought to be paid for idling, when others work hard.

Wor. No! no!   [*They resume their work.*

Gal. (sulkily carrying one small piece of wood). I'll drink a week for this, Sundays and all.

Rob. Always drink, drink,—these men study nothing else. If they would only think of the mischief it causes them. *(to* ARMAND *who has returned to the counting house).* The boats are cleared, sir.

Cla. Thanks to your example, Robert; I fear you work too much—sit down, pray.

Rob. (sits on a log by the counting house door). Bless you, Ma'mselle, for your kindness and consideration. A good word helps a man on with his toil, cheers his spirits, and makes hard work light—it comes like a refreshing breeze on his heated brow—a sweet reward for labour.

Mar. (in the archway). Some one wishes to see the wood piles, Monsieur?

Arm. Come with me, Robert.   [*They hasten out* c.

Cla. I'm surprised my father has not written to-day?

Mad. D. This will be the first time he ever returned home without giving notice.

Cla. He may be detained longer at Burgoyne than he expected.

Mad. D. You speak of his return as a matter of indifference. Yet he is very fond of you.

Cla. Heaven is my witness that I *dearly* love him. He is not a man that makes a display of his affections. A word, a look of tenderness from him makes me happy.

Mad. D. I often doubt your affection.

Cla. Why?

Mad. D. The excessive attention bestowed on Robert. I cannot understand the preference you show him. You quite forget what *you* are, and *he* is.

Cla. True, I do forget, his rude manners and want of education which shocks you so much, but I do not forget his good and honest heart when I was a child, a mere infant—he fondled me in his arms—sharing my sorrows—partaking my childhood's pleasures—he was my confidant—defender. If I committed a fault, who, but Robert, gained my pardon? Often my father's forgiving kiss would have been withheld but for him. Can you wonder then at a love that grew as I grew, and will last in spite of his rough manners and coarse coat. It is the *heart* I value—a jewel more precious than all the world's refined hypocrisy.

Mad. D. Well, I can't understand it—it's a mystery to me still.

Cla. (smiles). A mystery! Is gratitude for affection and devotion so rare? Listen—three years ago, before you were with us, I was suffering from a fatal fever. The doctors gave up all hopes of saving me. Robert never quitted my room, day or night—watching—anticipating every wish—indulging my caprices. My father, engrossed by business, seldom saw me, all was left to Robert. To him I owe existence. The knowledge (young as I was) of *one* heart that *really* loved me, cheered and comforted me. On my recovery, he brought me fruit and flowers, and at the head of our workmen came to wish me joy. My father evinced no care for me. All the love I experienced came from Robert. This may account for the familiarity you fancy misplaced, but that I am proud of.

Mad. D. It's quite natural. *(aside).* I know her father's not pleased with it though.

[MUSIC.—*A bell rings.* CLARISSE *and* MADAME DONTEL *exeunt into house,* L. *A number of* WOMEN *and* CHILDREN *enter* c. *with dinner for the* WORKMEN, *in jugs, basins. The* WORKMEN *all form into groups eating and drinking.* GALON'S *son, a ragged boy brings him a small jug.*

Gal. I've done. Who'll drink with me? I'll spend a sou.

Bob. (*his son*). I will, like a fish.

Mar. Remember, Robert won't let you idle in work hours.

Gal. He's a fool with his morality and fine words. Let him look to his own affairs. A nice man—I remember him twenty years back, and his tricks.

Mar. You had better tell him so.

Gal. So I will. Let him come and I'll—I'll—

ROBERT re-enters. C.

Rob. What?

Gal. Toss you for a bottle up and down.   [*Offers to toss.*

Mar. You were going to tell of some tricks of master Robert's, twenty years since.

Gal. I—I— Nonsense. Dont—it's a secret.

Rob. It *is* a secret, but one, since *he* has alluded to it, that shall be revealed. Then you will learn and judge if I am not right when I advise you to abandon drink. Twenty years back I was what you now are, a workman. I had a wife that loved me, and a child, a pretty little innocent eighteen months old. We laboured hard—we might have done well but for a fault, mine was more than a fault—a vice—a sin—it proved our ruin, drinking! It drove me furious, impoverished my pocket, destroyed our happiness, plunged us into poverty and crime. One night, allured by the love of wine, I accompanied a party of my companions to a tavern. We were the best of friends, till the devil tempted us. A quarrel arose, blows ensued—one gave me the lie—my blood boiled in my veins—I was mad. I strove to reach the man that had insulted me ; I was struck on the head by several of the ruffians—infuriated by the blows—maddened with drink,—I seized a knife, and my opponent fell dead at my feet. [*Crosses to* L. *much agitated.*

Mar. (*to* GALON). Why pain him by alluding to this?

Rob. If it be a lesson to you, a warning, I am content. Never keep bad company ; mine condemned me to five years imprisonment in the galleys, and the loss of all that was dear to me.

Mar. Your wife?

Rob. Died before I obtained my release.

Mar. And the little girl?

Rob. I have no child—no daughter. I am alone in the world— alone!

Mar. Poor fellow! She is dead then?

Rob. Dead to all but me. (*aside, smiling.*) Not a word to Ma'amselle Clarisse. Quick, quick, to your work.

[MUSIC.—The WOMEN leave, &c., as above.

CLARISSE *and* MADAME DONTREL *re-enter from house,*
ARMAND following.

Cla. Have you the bills?

Arm. Yes, Ma'amselle, ten thousand francs to receive of Monsieur Duval.   [*Shows pocket-book.*

Cla. That, with the twelve thousand we have in the house, will do for all demands to-morrow.

Arm. Monsieur Martial desired me to say he would call to-day for a list of prices

Rob. Martial! That's the grand personage in glazed boots and kid gloves. He's often in the yard since master left. What's his purpose?

Cla. Wood, to build a large house, so he states.

Mad. D. He's a delightful man! So polite to the fair sex— he's a duck!

Rob. (aside). And you're a goose. The polish of his boots has won the old woman's heart.

Cla. You wont be late, Armand.

Arm. Not for worlds, if it would cause you uneasiness, Ma'amselle. *(taking her hand).*

Mad. D. (separating them). There, there, go about your business, its getting dark.

> [*Exit:* ARMAND *through arch;* CLARISSE *goes up the stage, and exit.*

That young man neglects his duty.

Rob. No, he does not—you dislike him, and for what?

Mad. D. Aye, for what, pray?

Rob. Interest—money. You favour M. Martial's visits. Not to purchase wood, but to talk to Clarisse, because he's rich. Mind what you're about.

Mad. D. And mind what you're about. I'll speak to your master. Talk to me! indeed, me! Paltry fellow!

> [*Noise of carriage heard.*

Mar. (without). Return in an hour.

Mad. D. His voice!

Rob. Mind, I say.

MONSIEUR MARITAL *enters,* C. *dressed in the first style ; he is foppish in the extreme.* ROBERT *sits on the log.*

Mar. Madame Dontel, I'm delighted to see you ; still charm-ing—always blooming. You are a perpetual spring, with smiles on your lips and fire in your eyes. On my honor, you're a perfect prodigy—a wonder.

Mad. D. (aside). Oh! what a magnificent creature!

> [*Curtseys.*

Mar. I dont perceive Ma'amselle Clarisse, is she visible ?

Rob. No, she's occupied.

Mar. Eh! *(eyeing him through glass).*

Rob. If you want timber, I can sell it.

Mar. I wish to see the mistress of the house.

Mad. D. You hear that *bear.*

Rob. I do bore. *(roughly).* I'll not lose sight of him.

[*Going up stage.*

Mad. D. Condescend to sit, sir, and I'll fetch my young lady. What a man! *(sighs).* Splendiferous.   [*Exit into house.*

Mar. (supposing himself alone). The moment I have sought for has arrived. *(He is moving towards the house. Stops, seeing* ROBERT). You can return to your work, my good man.

Rob. Can I? thank you; it aint polite to leave a gentleman alone. I'm here to keep you company.

Mar. (aside). Devil take him. *(aloud)* Do you treat all your customers thus?

Rob. There's so many sort of customers—some to buy— some to sell—odd customers—queer customers—you look like a queer one.

Mar. Fellow! *(aside).* Does he suspect?

Rob. Customers, that knowing the father's absent, come to mislead a young girl, and blind a foolish old woman. Fortunately there's a very fine dog, always loose, with sharp teeth, if he should bite you, do'nt blame me.

Mar. A dog!

Rob. Yes, and a rough one. If you mean wrong, do'nt come within my reach. I'm the dog, and bite d—d hard; look to it!

Mar. (smiling). My good friend ——

Rob. I'm no friend of yours.

Mar. Friend or enemy, favour me by leaving me! I wish to be alone, booby!

Rob. Booby! *(raises his hand).*

CLARISSE *and* MADEMOISELLE DONTEL *enters.*

Cla. Robert! What is this?

Mar. Nothing, Ma'amselle, I have had the misfortune to displease M. Robert, that is all.

Rob. Displease! You never pleased me!

Cla. I am surprised, Robert—do you wish to offend me? Pray be more respectful in future.

Rob. I obey, Ma'amselle, but for you —— *(aside, shaking his hand at* MARLIAL.*)*

Cla. I must beg you to excuse his temper, sir; he is honest and faithful.

Mar. No apologies—he's like all men of his class.

Mad. D. Great bears.

Mar. I should have been here before, but that your canal is so far from the fashionable part of the town, it's quite a voyage; but fatigue vanishes on beholding you. *(bows.)*

Mad. D. His words are like honey and sugar.

[*Folds up her work and enters house.*

Cla. This is the list of prices you wished for, Monsieur, but there are several little errors that I will correct, if you'll allow me.　　　　　　　　*[Exit into counting house,* S. E. R.

Mar. As you please, Ma'amselle. *(bows.)* I have but an instant. *(Takes a key from his pocket and runs to house door,* S. E. L. *Tries it in the lock.)* It fits. *(Replaces it in his pocket as* ARMAND *re-enters with a bag of silver.)*

Arm. (bows.) Your servant, Monsieur?

Mar. Ah, my young friend, good day.

Cla. (re-entering). You are soon returned.

Arm. Yes, Ma'amselle. I hurried home.

Mar. I should think so, with a treasure ! *(points to bag.)*

Arm. (to CLARISSE*).* I have brought seven of the ten thousand in notes.　　　　　　　　*[Entering the house.*

Mar. Your business requires considerable sums of money, I presume ?

Cla. Oh yes, sir, to-morrow I have to pay '20,000 francs. My father would die if a bill bearing his signature was not paid when presented.

Mar. I have heard much of his probity and honesty.

> *[She gives him the list. He goes up stage and examines it.* ARMAND *re-enters.*

Arm. Has he made the purchase ?

Cla. Not yet.

Arm. (aside). If he keep the promise he made me, I shall be the happiest of men.

Mar. (to CLARISSE*).* Every thing is very moderate. All prices. To-morrow I'll select the timber.

> JOHN, *his Tiger enters, gazing vacantly around* C.

Arm. Who do you want, pray ? *(It grows dark.)*

John. My master.

Mar. Is that you, John ? *(It gets darker).*

John. Yes, Mounseer, I'm tired of waiting.

Mar. This is an odd fellow that I brought from England— he's no fool !

John. (laughs.) I believe you, though I can't parley woos.

Mar. Have you executed my orders?

John. I've been to the great house, and your friends, the gentlemen, say, they shall expect you to-night.

Mar. Very well. *(to* ARMAND*).* This concerns you. Come to me at eleven, and I will introduce you to those that will promote your interest. Dont mention it here.

Arm. How can I thank you ?

Mar. Bring the carriage up.

John. Yes, my lord. *(aside).* Have you tried the key?

Mar. (kicking him aside). Silence, ass !

John. (screams). Oh !　　　　　　　　*[Runs out* C.

Mar. Adieu, Mademoiselle. To-morrow we shall conclude our bargain. Au revoir, Mons. Armand. *(aside).* The money's mine.   [*Exit* c.

Arm. What a gentleman he is !

Cla. We must think of closing the gates for the night, it grows late. (ROBERT *re-enters with a lantern*). Good night.

Rob. Good night, Ma'amselle. I'm going my round. All's safe.

[MUSIC.—CLARISSE *enters house. A light is seen at the window up stairs, and the door shut.* AR-MAND *beckons* ROBERT.

Arm. Robert, I must go out again.

Rob. At this time of night. You, who always keep good hours. *(shakes head).*

Arm. It is a matter of importance calls me, one that will procure me happiness and riches—to-morrow I will tell you all. *(Clock strikes ten).* I have just time to keep my appointment—lend me the key to let myself in.

Rob. (gives key). Mind and return early, the canal's a dangerous place. Good night, and be careful.

Arm. Never fear, thank you.

[MUSIC.—ARMAND *exit* c. ROBERT *closes* c. *gate.*

Rob. He's a good lad, and I'm sure one that confidence can be placed in; he's incapable of doing a bad action, or no key would he have had. I wish he was rich enough to marry Clarisse, they love each other fondly. I'll do all I can to assist them.

[MUSIC.—*He examines the yard and fastens gate; as he goes off a man's head appears looking over the wall—it is* JOHN, *now wearing a blouse and cap. A low whistle, and* PIPOD *scales the arch at back.* LOUCHON *descends from the timber stack.* JOHN *slides down the counting house roof, all very ragged.*

John. The old fellow's just left the yard—the money's there.

[*Points to house.*

Pip, You say Martial's sure of the key ? It fits ?

John. Like wax. They're all asleep—the young chap, Armand's out by Martial's invitation; he's going to do something for him. *(laughs).* Ha! ha!

[MUSIC.—JOHN *tries key in door, it opens.*—PIPOD *and he enter, and return instantly with pocket-book and bag.*

It's ours! All right. (*Footsteps heard*). Run! run!

> [*Closes door and runs into dog kennel with money.* PIPOD *hides behind wood.* LOUCHON *climbs up gate.* ROBERT *re-enters with lantern from* R. *to* L.—*pauses.* JOHN *peeps out.* PIPOD *and* LOUCHON *peep from the wood stack.*

SCENE II.—*The Rue de Coq. A garret gaily decorated with French paper. Door in flat, and a small fire place—stove.* MELANIE, *a Grisette, enters singing with a basket,* D. *in* F.

Mel. (*taking off her bonnet and shawl*). What a delicious dinner I will have. (*Runs to* R. *for a table and two stools*). There, now my drawing room furniture's arranged for the day. What a little glutton I am? Salad, bread, fruit, and chickweed for my birds. I refuse myself none of the elegancies of life. (*sits*). Let me see, my 30 sous a day, and I can't earn more by working half the night—(*sighs*)—must keep three of us—myself, a blind goldfinch, and a petite lame mouse. (*counts her fingers*). 30, 10, 20, and 20s. 30.—No.--No.—I don't mean that. (*counts quickly*).{ Bread, four sous.—Milk, nothing—I don't drink it. Six for salads—I adore salads, they're so easily dressed—Three for butter, and all the rest for fun, dancing, and singing. Meat's too dear to eat, besides it makes my boudoir smell like a kitchen, and I musn't spoil my paradise—it's only seven stories high, beautifully papered, and always two pots of flowers in the windows at a time. I ought to be happy—I am. The happiest girl in Paris—and one of the genteelest, especially in my blue Levantine dress. That, I only wear on Sunday. My polka boots, and imitation silk shawl—the men stare at me as I pass, and whisper " what a beauty !"—" Twig her symmetry !"—" Oh, those ancles !"—" Fine animal, pon honor !" Then I laugh and trip by. When Barbillon was in good circumstances he used to take me to the boulevards and the barriers, to dances, and fêtes, and always left me to pay for him. Billiards and fine company ruined his prospects. Instead of attending to me, I attended to him. The only thing he ever treated me to was neglect. He has never been here since I lent him my money box to look at, with two francs in it, saved up for rent. He's a true town lover, preferring noise to solitude; the glare of the lamps to the beauty of the country; the mud of the streets to the verdure of the flowery meadows; its scorching pavements to the fresh velvet moss of the wood paths, perfumed with violets; the suffocating dust of the barriers to the waving of the yellow golden corn. My thoughts always fondly linger amid the scenes of childhood—Ma belle Normandie.

SONG.

'Midst gay and splendid palaces,
  Still for thee I pine.
Home of my childhood's fancy,
  Land of the purple vine.
Others may boast of riches;
  'Tis yours to be free.
Land of my heart's devotion,
  Ma belle Normandie!

Your children's a virtue,
  Ne'er yet bought or sold;
A pleasure, far surpassing,
  All the worldling's gold.
Blest liberty and honour,
  Your watchword ever be,
Land of my heart's devotion,
  Ma belle Normandie!

[*A bell heard.*

Mel. That's my hare's foot. I hope it isn't the landlord come to ask me for the rent again. Its in the money box.

[*Another ring.*

Bar. (*whispering outside* R.) Melanie, my only love.

Mel. Barbillon! who's there?

Bar. A drowned rat *ringing* himself dry (*rings bell*).

Mel. (*opens the door,* BARBILLON *enters very ragged, muddy, and dripping wet.*) I don't know you, sir.

Bar. I should wonder if you did: my respectable mamma wouldn't in this plight.

Mel. Where's my box?

Bar. Sold.

Mel. And the money?

Bar. Spent.

Mel. Wretch! it was to pay my rent.

Bar. Pardon, my angelic, my venerable mother was ravenous, and my three lame aunts voracious, I had sold everything, my furniture, clothes, toothpick, everything, reduced myself to my garters; what could I do? Nature struggling, knocking against the door, four beloved relatives singing out for food and water—the cruel landlord cut off the cock.

Mel. You are speaking the truth.

Bar. Could I utter a falsehood? (*takes her hand*)

Mel. How have you lived since I saw you last?

Bar. On suction.

Mel. Where?

Bar. Under water. I've been diving in the canal for a crust, wandering on the banks, trying to persuade people to throw money in for me to fetch out. Sometimes I pushed a child in on the sly, then jumped in to save him. This brought in a few sous—but even that failed in time. One infernal day I pushed in a boy as usual, brought him out, expecting a reward—and I got it from his father.

Mel. What?

Bar. A broken head—the old buffer saw me push him in. I've done little since—nobody cares about drowning themselves now except the police, and they do it in drink.

Mel. Why not try something honest?

Bar. I never learnt. I was hired for a perambulating pill box one day, but when I asked for money my master, a quack, offered me physic. (MELANIE *laughs.*) I tried an industrious flea after, it wouldn't *bite.* The arts have fallen—I shall speculate and try a few shares in a new line.

Mel. What line, pray?

Bar. A *line* with a long *hook*—the unlimited extension, ask no question, broad or narrow guage Great Truck Railway. I've written for 200,000 shares already.

Mel. Why you can't pay a sou.

Bar. I don't want—*selling's* my object, not *buying.* The shares mine I turn them into gold—then for the carnival, dance, theatres, love and sugar plums—vive la Bagatelle.

Mel. But is this right?

Bar. Can it be wrong—everybody does it. All the world's running on a rail! No standing still—the steam's up, and if men didn't speculate now to let it off, their boilers would burst.

Mel. If you become so rich you'll soon forget me.

Bar. Never. I may be a thoughtless, idle scamp, but not heartless; and if I thought I should ever be scoundrel enough to forget you, the kind affectionate girl that had assisted me in adversity I'd jump into the canal, and d—n me if I'd pull myself out again.

Mel. My own Barbillon (*runs to him*).

Bar. My Melanie (*embraces her*) how nice it is—I wish we could afford to do it often. What have you got to eat? I get nothing but drink.

Mel. (arranges contents of basket.) A salad.

Bar. Divine! the doctors advise salad in the spring (*sits and eats.*)

Mel. Bread.

Bar. Sumptuous! What to follow?

Mel. Nothing.

Bar. That'll help to fill up.

Mel. We must fancy it a good dinner and be contented.

Bar. What's in the saucepan?

Mel. Water, hot.

Bar. Oh! I'm used to it cold (*the bell rings*).

Mel. Hush !

Bar. (*with his mouth full*) **W**ho is it ?   I'm jealous.

Mel. (*peeps*). Its my landlord—he wants his rent.

Bar. Let him want on (*bell rings and knocks*).

Voice. Ma'amselle Melanie are you in ?

Bar. (*in a gruff voice*) No, she's out.

Voice. Who are you.

Bar. Her mother.

Voice. I've called for my rent.

Bar. Call again to-morrow.

Voice. (*shakes door*) I won't be put off any more, if she doesn't pay I'll seize the furniture.

Mel My beautiful saucepan.

Bar. You will, eh ?

Voice. Every stick (BARBILLON *opens door,* GROS BŒUF, *a fat man stands in the door way*) The money, Madame, pay or I'll have it all.

Bar. You shall, old alligator (*knocks his hat over his eyes and pushes him to the door*) take it (*throws the stool after him,* MELANIE *laughs, then the table, he calls for aid* BARBILLON *catches up the saucepan and pours hot water over him, he roars out and tumbles down stairs.*) Victory ! Victory !

(*Flourishes   saucepan   and   runs   off   embracing* MELANIE.

SCENE III.—*The canal with street running up the stage* L. *in which is an arch leading to the wood yard, adjoining a wineshop. A bridge extends over the canal at back. Trees* R. *up stage. A large boat is on the canal with a number of women washing, persons are passing and repassing. When scene opens, it is daybreak. Workmen arriving.* MUSIC. GALON *lolling against a post* L. *smoking.* MARTIN *passing from* L.

Mar. Its six o'clock, aint you going to work ? (*enters yard.*)

Gal. Not till my pipe's out.

ROBERT *enters from the arch.*

Rob. You're a quarter behind time again.

Gal. (*sulkily*) Always hunting me ! Ugh, you old tormenter of innocence.   [*Exit into yard.*

Rob. Past six and Armand not returned yet. I've been waiting for him all night ; what has happened to the lad ? Can he have deceived me with his affair of importance ? I hope he's not fallen into bad company, for that may affect Clarisse's future welfare.

ARMAND *enters over the bridge* L. *to* R. *timidly.*

Arm. Thank Heaven, I'm at home at last. **Robert!**

Rob. Yes, looking for your return. Is this keeping good hours ? What have you been doing ?

Arm. You've been uneasy doubtless.

Rob. For your sake, that's all. Where have you been all night ?

Arm. Don't ask me ; be sure of this, not in mischief.

Rob. (*shakes his head*) Young man ! out all night and not in mischief. Go to work, go *(crosses to* R.)

Arm. It is evident you suspect me, let me explain. I adore Clarisse, you know it, but what hope have I, a poor clerk to her father ? None. Fortunately a gentleman has taken an interest in my behalf, and promises a situation that may bring me fifteen thousand francs a year.

Rob. This is all very well, but why stay out ?

Arm. I went to my friend's last evening, he insisted on my remaining.

Rob. May I ask his name ?

Arm. Marshall.

Rob. What the ape in glazed boots—what brings him here think you ?

Arm. Business to purchase.

Rob. Moonshine! Its Clarisse he comes after—are you blind ?

Arm. Impossible ! If he seeks her hand why profess to be my friend ?

Rob. To make a dupe of you.

Arm. When Monsieur Laroche returns, I'll declare my love for Clarisse—you will aid me ?

Rob. With all my heart, boy. Go in and change your coat and get into the counting-house, I wouldn't have it known that you'd been out all night for the world. Be quick and careful no one sees you, especially Madame Dontel, she's all eyes.

Arm. (shaking his hand) My good friend.

[*Exit into yard* R.

Rob. I don't much fancy this sudden friendship of Martial, why does he offer to assist him ?

BARBILLON *crosses the bridge* L. *to* R.

Bar. Good morning, Monsieur.

Rob. Barbillon.

Bar. Yes ; I've come to buy some timber. I'm going into the Lucifer match trade—diving won't do any longer, so I'll try the matches —a light business suits me.

Rob. I fear you've been leading a sad life, my lad.

Bar. Not I, its the life leading me—I'm obliged to follow it. I pushed a man into the canal just now, hoping to get something for pulling him out, after diving to the bottom for him he had no money in his pockets.   Nothing prospers; if I pick up a silver spoon it turns out pewter.

MARTIN, GALON, *and workmen enter from* L.

Gal. Huzza! I've won six bottles.

Rob. Again.

Gal. Its our quarter for rest ; won't you take a drop with us ?

Bar. I'll drink for him.

Gal. No, no.   I hope Monsieur Robert will join us in one cup for good fellowship.

Rob. I never drink,

Bar. Don't press him.

[MARTIAL *and* JOHN *cross the bridge, at the same time,* CLARISSE *enters from the yard* R.

Cla. Any tidings of my father's boat ?

Rob. It will be here early, Ma'amselle.

Mar. (approaching) I'm glad to hear it, my business will soon be arranged then.

Cla. You are early, Monsieur.

Mar. I seldom sleep late.

John. (aside) He's always wide awake.

Mar. Besides I wish to purchase of your father the moment he arrives. *(aside)* They suspect nothing.

Enter MONSIEUR JOSEPH, U. E. L.

Jos. Good morning, Ma'amselle.

Cla. Good morning, Monsieur, the money's quite ready, 20,000 francs,—you'll find Armand in the counting-house. — *(he goes in).*

Bar. (who has been talking to the workmen) Yes, there's a gang of thieves about the canal.

John (trembling) Oh lord!

Mar. Thieves! where ?

Bar. That's what I want to know. If I could lay my hands on them—*(placing his hand on* JOHN.*)*

John. Don't, you tickle.

Arm. (is heard within) Robbed! plundered! *(runs on pale and alarmed)* Ma'amselle Clarisse we have been robbed, the money's gone.

Cla. What !

Omnes. Gone.

Arm. The lock of the chest forced—the pocket-book stolen!

Cla. Good heavens ! My father will never forgive us.

Rob. Let us search. Some clue may be found to this mystery.

Cla Do, do, for mercy's sake.

[MUSIC.—CLARISSE *and* ROBERT *exeunt* R.

Bar. I said there were thieves about. If we catch them?

Gal. We'll hang 'em.

John. (aside). My throat. *(rubs it).*

Mar. I regret this untoward circumstance for your sake, my young friend.

Gal. How master'll swear! Let's search for the thieves, we'll drown them. Come, Monsieur Armand, come.

Omnes. Yes, yes.

[MUSIC.—*Exeunt into yard dragging* ARMAND.

John. I'm very ill. *(trembles).* Oh!

Mar. You left no traces behind that may betray us?

[PIPOD *steals on over the bridge, he whistles low.*

Mar. Fool! Why do you come here?

Pipod. We've found something. These family papers in the pocket-book, besides the money *(gives papers).* I thought, you'd like 'em.

Mar. Run, if you are seen—

John. We are dished. (PIPOD *steals off.* ROBERT *returns).*

Mar. Is there any trace left?

Rob. Devil a bit, they've managed too cleverly.

[CLARISSE, JOSEPH, ARMAND, *and* MADAME DO
TEL *re-enter.*

Cla. (speaks while fastening her bonnet, agitated). Give me your bill, sir. I'll go to our bank, it must be paid instantly. My father's credit shall not suffer. Try to collect some money, Armand, from the customers. All can be paid. *(to* MARTIAL). Your pardon, sir, but I must leave you to attend to this unfortunate affair.   [*Exit* L.

[*The* WORKMEN *re-enter from yard and exeunt into
wine shop.* T. E. L.

Arm. What will become of me!

Rob. Courage, lad, you talked of good friends. Perhaps this gentleman will prove one and assist you?

Mar. Willingly. Point out the way.

Rob. By lending him the money.

John. (aside). Hookey! Some of its mine.

Mar. I—I.—Hem!

Rob. Yes, you—didn't you promise him 15,000 francs a year? Pay him a year and a half in advance, that'll just do it, and prevent master's accusing him.

Mar. The situation I alluded to, is gone, I regret to say.

Rob. To be sure it is. *(laughs)*. These are your fine power-ful friends? You are a rich man, sir; this money won't hurt you. (MARTIAL *shakes his head*). Why what a fellow you must be to raise his hopes for nothing—a vain boaster.

Mar. Mind your words fellow.

John. *(aside)* Don't, don't, he'll murder us both.

[*All the* WORKMEN *stand at the wine shop door.*

Rob. You kept him from home all night, now this money's lost——

Mar. There are numbers of workmen employed, may they not have ——

Rob. Stop! Don't you say a word against them, or I'll knock you into the canal! No, no, it's not the poor honest workman, it's *those* that never work.

Mar. (laughs). Do you dare?

Rob. I dare speak the truth, and defend those who's living depends on the good opinion of their fellow men. What have they to rely on but character? If that is taken, loss of em-ployment must follow; then comes poverty, disgrace, and crime. Your fine coat protects you from these dangers, and my hand shall shield them from your slander.

Wor. Huzza! Leave him, Robert, you *shall* take a cup with us now, brave Robert. *(they force him into the wine shop).* Only one!

Bar. Accuse us! Bah! I'm ashamed of you.

[*Exit into wine house* R.

John. (to MARTIAL). Let us go.

Mar. And by so doing create suspicion. No! no! We'll look at the pocket-book. *(opens it).*

John. Let's keep all, and give the others none?

Mar. You hurt my feelings, —our honour is ——

John. All smoke. *(aside).* I'll keep my eye on him.

Mar. (examining papers—aside). What's this! La Roche, passenger on board the Rodin, for Havre, and come from Antillas, 1827. *(hastily concealing papers).* Great heaven! I saw him die on the coast of Guinea! Is the dead returned?

John. Is there anything good?

Mar. For nothing.

[*A noise in wine house,* R.

Rob. Let me pass.

Bar. Oh! I've lost my nose. Oh! oh!

Voices. Stop, stop.

[ROBERT *rushes out excited, followed by the workmen.*

Rob. He dared to insinuate we were robbers! There he is, still watching the place. He wants Ma'amselle Clarisse too—*(advances to* MARTIAL)—Monsieur, fine gentleman?

Mar. Well!

John. Well!

Rob. (*crosses to* L.) Silence, ape! (*throws him across the stage*). It is with your master I talk.

Bar. (*knocking his hat over his eyes*). Silence, ape!

Mar. Beware, Master Robert, the gallies, a second time.

[*whispers.*

Rob. Scoundrel! Why allude to that? (*raises his hand*).

Mar. I am armed. (*shews pistol*).

[ROBERT *is forced back.* MARTIAL *and* JOHN *retreat*

John. Let's call the guard, and shoot the old buffalo.

Mar. You shall repent this outrage, ruffian!

[*They exit over bridge.*

Bar. What a pity wine makes him so wild.

Rob. Who made me drink?

Bar. Don't say it was me.

Gal. (*aside*). I plead guilty to that.

Rob. It's unkind to expose a man like me to this infirmity. (*with feeling*). This recalls all my misery—the image of wife and child rise in judgment against me. Why tempt me?

[*A boat appears on the canal.*—CLARISSE *re-enters. The workmen run to canal.*

Gal. Master! Master!

Bar. The master! Won't the mistress catch it? The lost money—

Cla. Robert beg the men not to mention our loss to my father—I have obtained the money.

[MUSIC.—*The boat advances gently—the lock opening—mast rises.* LAROCHE *on deck guiding the boat with boat hook.* ARMAND *enters from the yard.*

Cla. (*to him*) When you have seen my father, run and pay the bill, here's the money, I'll manage the rest (*gives notes*). Pray don't tremble thus, he will suspect something, and his rage will be terrible.

La R. (*from boat.*) Make fast the boat.

Gal. Alls right.

[*Music. Fastens it to a post; a plank is placed from the boat to the quay,* LA ROCHE *crosses it.*

Rob. Glad to see you, sir.

La R. Are you?

Cla. I'm so rejoiced you've returned safe, dear father.

La R. I dare say you are. Come here (*to* ROBERT,) has all been right in the yard (ROBERT *bows*). Unload the boat, and be quick about it *(the men unload it.)* Clraisse ! *(she goes to his* L. MADAME DONTEL, *his* R. *having just entered.*

Mad. D. I hope your health is the same ?

La R. I havn't changed it.   I trust, sir, *(to* ARMAND) you have done *your* duty, and proved yourself worthy of my confidence.

Mad D. (aside) He has nicely.

Cla. (aside) Should he discover him, *(aloud).*   Won't you rest yourself after your fatigue ?

La R. When I'm tired.   I must look to these rascals, no shirking there—quick *(to men, going up.)*

Cla. Now run and fetch the bills—I will plead for you.

[*Exit* ARMAND *into yard* L.

MARTIAL *re-enters on bridge.*

Mar. (down R.*)* Laroche has arrived I perceive. Those features ! the look !—it must be my man.

Cla. (R. *seeing* MARTIAL) Father, this is our new customer, Monsieur Martial, he wishes to purchase a pile of wood for building.

La R. If the gentleman will do us the favour of calling to-morrow.

[CLARISSE *talks to* MADAME DONTEL.

Mar. That will be too late, to-night I must see you alone, choose the hour and place.

La R. What do you mean, sir ?

Mar. It means that we have met before, Pierre Bernard, pirate and murderer *(whispers.)*

La R. (starts) Betrayed! who and what are you ?

Mar. That you shall learn to-night—name the place.

La R. In my cabin, on board the boat St. Nicholas.

Mar. The time ?

La R. Ten.

Mar. I shall be punctual *(Music—turns to talk to* CLARISSE.*)*

La R. The fiends seize him.

[JOHN *appears on the bridge, followed by guards.*

John That's the ruffian in the grey whiskers, he threatened to kill us, secure him.

Bar. (who is on the bridge) I will *(seizing* JOHN, *throwing him into the canal and jumping after him, the workmen shout and run to canal.)*

Mars. The miscreant ! my servant will be drowned. *(aside)* I hope so.

Rob. No, no, he's climbing the bank.

Mar. I demand his arrest.

> [*Music. The guards advance, the workmen endea-
> vour to stop them ; they charge, the* WORKMEN
> *run, at this time, the* WASHERWOMEN *from
> boat all rush out and pelt the guards with wet
> clothes, the* WORKMEN *rally. A struggle takes
> place very rapid, the guards are beaten and
> some thrown into the canal.* BARBILLON *runs
> on bridge.*

Bar. I won't jump in to save them (*crows like a cock*).

> [*Workmen shout. Picture. Drums beat, people on
> all sides.* CLARISSE *clings to* ROBERT, JOHN
> *crawls in, covered with mud, and falls in* MAR-
> TIAL'S *arms.*

END OF ACT I.

ACT II.

SCENE I.—*The cabin of the St. Nicholas, A table and two stools, one over a trap. A small closet,* R. *Cabin window in flat,* T. E. L. *A door leading to the deck,* S. E. L. *Steps and door. Music.*—LAROCHE *enters with a lantern down steps, hangs it up, then sits.*

Lar. At 10, Monsieur Martial will be here. Who and what is he? I thought there was no living soul in Europe that knew Pierre Bernard. Now, after twenty year's security, a stranger that I had never seen before, pronounces that name in my ears. How could he have learnt it? Where? And, knowing, why demand this secret interview? But, what have I to fear? With a reputation so firmly established! I can prove he must be mistaken in my resemblance, and that Laroche, the merchant, is not the pirate, Bernard. Yet, when his eyes were fixed on me, I felt we had met before. *(clock strikes nine).* There is an hour to wait. The delay is welcome. To account for the fear I have is impossible; my spirits sink, and I feel as if something serious, some danger, hung over me. If so, I can quit Paris for ever. At all events, it will be well to prepare for the worst—in ten minutes I can remove all my money from the bankers.

Rob. (without, D. S. E. L.*)* You can't enter, I tell you.

Gal. We must.

Lar. (opens door). What's the meaning of this noise?

Rob. Galon and the workmen want to see you, but I knew you didn't wish to be disturbed.

Lar. Let them come in. (ROBERT *beckons).*

GALON *enters timidly—the workmen peep in at the door,* ROBERT *comes down* R

Why have you left your work?

Gal. It's nine o'clock, sir.

Lar. You can go then.

Gal. It's been a hard day's work, and we're very dry.

Lar. Oh, you want something to drink, eh?

Gal. Uncommon. (LAROCHE *gives money).*

Lar. Divide this.

Gal. We will, master, and drink your health; if you please, every year the canal merchants give their workmen a dance and a fête, it's your turn next?

Lar. I will do as others do.

Gal. Huzza! Perhaps you'll give us a little money in advance?

Lar. To encourage idleness?

Omnes. No, sir!

Lar. This time I'll try you; but I shall watch you narrowly.

[*Goes to cupboard, unlocks it, and lakes out money.*

Gal. (to the others). We shall have it, boys; he's in a capital humour.

Mar. And you've done nothing to deserve it.

Gal. I work hard. I've smoked three pipes already and drank four glasses of cognac. I tried a fifth but my spirit was gone.

Lar. (returning). Robert, you'll tell me who has not worked properly. *(gives money).* Now take yourselves off; in five minutes let the boat be cleared of every soul. Robert, you wait for me.   [*Exit up steps.*

Omnes. Thank you, sir.

Gal. Huzza boys! Now for a cask of wine. Bottles be —— Hum!

[*Workmen laugh and sing without—dancing the Polka—their steps heard heavily.*

Rob. Give them money for drinking—he can't be in his right senses—he that hates all enjoyment.

[BARBILLON *pops his head in at the centre window and whistles the polka.*

Rob. Are you in the water?

Bar. Not exactly. I'm on a raft, watching a fat man I have just pushed in to pull him out again. There he is, how he rolls about—hallo! he's going—I've got him now—why its only a wig, The fat chap's gone but the wig is saved. *(throws wig in wet).* Lend me a cord?

Rob. You can't enter.

Bar. I must—the raft's slipping from me. Oh, your hand, or I shall follow the fat chap, under the boat. *(climbs into the boat).*

Rob. What a rascal! You can't stay here.

Bar. I've stay'd here often before—entered by the cabin window in the river by the night.

Rob. If Mr. Laroche catches you?

Bar. He won't—I saw him hurrying over the bridge. It's a snug place, eh? Not so comfortable as it looks. Folks do say your master deals in other things besides wood—smuggling. What does he want with voyages to Flanders?

Rob. Evil reports, without foundation. *(footsteps heard above).* He is returning.

c

Bar. (runs to window, L.*)* Give me a leg up.

CLARISSE *enters* L. *door. accompanied by* ARMAND.

Cla. Is my father here ?

Rob. No, Ma'mselle, but he won't be long.

Cla. We wish to see him alone.

Rob. I am here by his orders.

Bar. And I, without. Au revoir, Ma'amselle. I know good breeding better than to intrude. *(bows).* Bon jour, Monsieur.   [BARBILLON *ascends steps.*

Arm. What a distressing task have you imposed on yourself, Clarisse. I entreat you to abandon this project. I will explain my misfortune to Mr. Laroche myself. Let me encounter his anger, alone.

Cla. No, my father is just—though a severe man, he cannot hold you responsible for another's crime, even presuming your absence to have caused his loss. He will excuse—pardon it—and I shall be doubly gratified in having obtained it.

Bar. (runs down). He's coming in a devil of a passion. I saw him push Madame Dontel aside. I was in hopes he'd have knocked her over. What a fine diver the old lady would make.   [*Runs to window and climbs up.*

Rob. You are going.

Bar. To my native element,—spirits and water. The *spirits* are *here*, the water *there*. I always mix 'em.

[*Jumps out—a splash heard.*

La R. (without) Why do you come here? where's Clarisse? *(very loud, entering* L.*)* So, madam, it appears that during my absence I've been robbed, plundered—money, family papers of vast importance, letters, are stolen from my chest, and you were left to guard it.

Mad. D. (who has followed LA ROCHE *to* CLARISSE*)* He has just been to his banker's and learnt all.

La R. What have you to say to this, sir? you, whom I kept from charity *(to* ARMAND.*)*

Cla. Father I am—

La R. I did not address myself to you. *(Crosses to* ARMAND.*)*

Rob. (aside) Don't irritate him.

La R. You were absent from home, I learn, when the robbery took place.

Arm. I—I—

La R. Do not lie. I know you passed the night out, Madame Dontel saw you steal home at six in the morning. Is this your vigilance, your duty to me, sir?

Arm. I know I have done wrong.

La R. What satisfaction is that to me ? Where is my money ? Begone, sir, never let me see you again. (*crosses to* R).

[ARMAND *turns away,* CLARISSE *stops him.*

Rob. Monsieur La Roche.

La R. I won't hear you.

Cla. Listen to me, dear father, you have often told me I should inherit a great fortune, let the riches you promised go towards this loss, keep it ; I shall be content never to marry but to work for you, all the indulgence I beg is forgiveness for Armand.

La R. Instead of caring for him, you'd better care for yourself—he goes (*waves his hand*) out of my sight.

[ARMAND *and* MADAME DONTEL *exeunt at the door* L. CLARISSE *follows in tears.*

Cla. Father, have mercy.

La R. Fool, begone. *(she exits sobbing).*

Rob. She's unable to bear this harshness.

Lar. (*throwing himself on a seat,* R. *leaning his head on his hand*) My papers gone—this mysterious interview—there's some connection—a fatal secret.

Rob. I can't stand it—it's no use, sir, I must speak.

La R. I've no time to listen—to-morrow.

Rob. To night—now.

La R. Are you not afraid of irritating me ?

Rob. Afraid ! I'm neither an old woman or a child, but a man who will be heard. You've not kept your promises with me.

La R. (*calmly*) Indeed !

Rob. (L.) No. It is now nearly twenty years since I was a condemned criminal, you met me at Malines, taking leave of my child, a poor thing two years old, that was going to a public charity. You said you'd just returned from America where you lost your child, about the same age as mine, and offered to take her to give her your name and fortune, care, tenderness, happiness,—you promised all. I consented—making only only one condition, that she should never know that she was the daughter of a criminal.

La R. I remember.

Rob. My heart was breaking—my character lost for ever, and to hide my shame from my own child, I agreed to all, as I was dragged away chained to the companions of my infamy, you held in your arms all, all I held dear on earth—my little little child *(sobs.)*

La R. Havn't I kept my word ? She is well educated—will be rich.

Rob. It isn't of that I complain—you've done much.

La R. And what did you do? Instead of flying your country for ever on leaving prison, as you promised, you were seen constantly prowling about the house that contained your daughter, and with tears in your eyes, begged me to take you in.

Rob. I couldn't help it. Nature led me—my heart's blood, feelings, hope, life, were shut up there.

La R. I gave you work.

Rob. And you've no cause to complain—your interest is mine.

La R. What do you require?

Rob. Nothing for myself, it is for her—you're too severe to her, too harsh.

La R. Not more so than to others.

Rob. So much the worse for them, but my poor girl feels it—never a kind look or tender kiss. Just now she wanted to plead for Armand. Its hard and unjust to send him away.

La R. I had my reason—he loved Clarisse, Madame Dontel told me so.

Rob. She's an old witch—what if he does? She loves him.

La R. So much the worse for her, she shall never marry him. Why do you interfere? you've nothing to do with it.

Rob. Not with the happiness of my girl?

La R. She's no longer yours. *(aside, looking at watch).* Ten—I must get rid of him. I have some bills to examine, leave me; we'll speak of Armand another time—to-morrow.

Rob. Be it so. I knew you would relent. Good night, sir.

[*Exit at door.* MARTIAL *is seen watching on the steps.*

La R. I was fearful the stranger might come.

Mar. *(cooly)* He is here. (LA ROCHE *starts*). No one saw me enter. I heard talking and drew back.

[LA ROCHE *closes door and window.*

La R. Now, sir.

Mar. Now, Pierre Bernard.

La R. My name is La Roche; utter the name of Bernard again and I'll turn you out.

Mar. Four words will alter your determination—" The Eagle, the Roden."

La R. *(aside)* He knows me. What of the Roden.

Mar. She was a fine vessel, frequented the African coast, a pirate—a slaver. In the year 1827, the Roden was let to a Captain Pierre Bernard by a colonist, named La Roche; he sailed for France with his infant daughter to claim a rich inheritance due to her. Is it true?

La R. You learnt this from my papers. I have been

robbed of 20,000 francs, the authorities are searching—you are the thief.

Mar. (*coolly*) That's true. Now I'll tell you something that was not in the papers. A dreadful storm arose during the voyage of the Roden to France. She was driven on the banks of Newfoundland. Laroche, his child, and Pierre Bernard left the vessel in a boat and reached the shore. The Roden struck, all hands perished but one—a boy—the waves washed him ashore—there he saw the child dead, and the colonist falling beneath the blows of a poignard. The waves served as a tomb to both victims. The colonist was La Roche —the assassin, Pierre Bernard, yourself.

La R. (*starting*) Speak lower.

Mar. The witness of this horrible tragedy concealed himself, trembling from fear and cold, among the rocks.

La R. It was Gaspard.

Mar. At your service (*bows*).

La R. You escaped then—returned to France ?

Mar. To serve my friends.

La R. And you dare recall this to me in my own boat, alone—have you no fear ?

Mar. None. I have two friends with me.

La R. (*alarmed*) Where

Mar. Here. (*shows pistols*).

La R. What is your object ?

Mar. Money.

La R. Much ?

Mar. As much as you can conveniently spare at a time.

La R. And the papers ?

Mar. Are useless; I can easily reveal all I know. (*gives papers.*)

La R. Let us be friends ; sit down. To seal it, we'll drink together. (*slaps him on the shoulder*).

Mar. With pleasure.

> [LA ROCHE *fetches from cupboard* U. E. R. *bottle and two glasses.*

La R. Drink. (*offers glass*).

Mar. After you. (*smiles*).

La R. You suspect me ?

Mar. How can I ? but politeness.

> [LA ROCHE *drinks, then* MARTIAL.

La R. Now tell me your demand ?

Mar. You're anxious to get rid of me.

La R. It will be better for both, my personal security is at stake. Name the hour—another glass. (*pours it out*) Your health.

Mar. Thanks. (*drinks*) Now I am yours.

La R. You are—adieu !

> [*Music. Touches a secret spring under the table,
> the plank gives way under* MARTIAL *and he
> disappears through the stage. A loud cry heard
> from* CLARISSE, *who is seen on the stairs, she
> tries to cling to the balustrade for support, trem-
> bling violently, and gradually sinks.*

La R. (*turning and running to her*). She has seen all—the
canal silences his tongue for ever ; if she dare breathe, death
follows.

Cla. (*recovering, shudders.* LAROCHE *approaches her*). No !
no ! do not touch me ——

> [*Raises his hand and advancing.*

> [*Supports herself with difficulty ; her face averted
> from* LA ROCHE. *He extends his hands to assist
> her, at the touch she falls, with a low cry of dis-
> gust and terror, at his feet. Scene closes.*

SCENE II.—*A Street,*

MELANIE *enters,* R. *crying.*

Mel. Oh ! oh ! oh ! I'm a deceived feminine innocent. (*calls*).
Barbillon ! Where are you ? He's borrowed my purse, and
left me without a single sous. He's always betraying my confidence. Call this pleasure, it's all pain. Yesterday he played
me another shabby trick—he came in a hurry to ask me for
change for half a franc ; after he'd got the change, he said he
must owe me the half franc, for his mother wanted milk.
(*calls*). Barbillon ! To-day I gave him the money to pay for
a cab, and he spent it in lady's fingers. He's a brute !

AGATHA *enters.* L.

Aga. What do you want ?
Mel. If you please, ma'am, I want to find an honest man.
Aga. (*laughs*). You're too near sighted my love. [*Exit.* R.

> [*Loud laughing without. She looks off,* R.

Mel. The company are all coming ! Taking refreshments.
I must *take* myself off. Barbillon's got all my money. Oh !
oh ! I'm a ruined bankrupt. Nothing left but my beauty and
an old brass thimble.   [*Exit.* L.

> [*Music heard without, and loud laughing. All the
> workmen, wives, guests, dance on (a galop) in
> their best apparel.* R.

Aga. What a delicious treat.
Nin. All roses,

Mar. A glorious day! full of fun and sunshine.

GALON *and* BOBO *his son, dressed grotesquely in his father's coat, enter.* L. GALON *carries a guitar.*

The Workmon shout, Galon, Galon.

Gal. Yes? and here's my son and heir, so between us there is a gallon and a half.

[*Omnes laugh and shout.*

Gal. Your servant, gentlemen and ladies. (*to* BOBO). Bow you devil, and show your breeding. (BOBO *bows*). Waiter!

Bobo. (*calls*). Waiter!   [WAITER *runs on* U. E. L.

Gal. A glass of wine!

Bobo. Only one glass, there's *two* of us, pa! (*they laugh*).

Mar. Why didn't you come sooner?

Gal. That gentleman took so much time dressing his hair. I've brought the music with me. We'll have a mazourka and a polka.

Bobo I like a polka. (*dances a few steps*).

Gal. Where's the governor? Has he arrived, and Ma'am-selle Clarisse?

Mar. Not yet.

Gal. We'll receive him well when he does come,—such a fête as this deserves a hearty welcome.

Omnes. Yes, to be sure.

Bobo. I'll ask him to smoke a cigar and pay for it.

Aga. Let's have a dance?

Gal. I prefer a drink.

Aga. Is that your gallantry to the ladies? Shabby!

Bobo. Shabby! shabby!

[GALON *strikes his cracked guitar, and sings l'Amour !*
l'Amour! BOBO *imitates him.*

Mar. Choose your partners, lads.

Bobo. (*strutting up to a very tall woman*). This is mine! (*bowing*).

[*All shout.—A galop commences.—The waiter runs on,* F. E. L.

Wai. Dinner!

Gal. Hurra!

[*All run off,* F. E. L. BOBO *last, galloping with his tall partner.*

LA ROCHE *enters dejectedly.* R.

La R. (*pausing*). Why is Clarisse not here? It was my orders, ever since yesterday, she studiously seeks to avoid me—to see or speak to her is impossible, and I hear she's always in tears. That fellow, Robert, never leaves her. He must go, with his violence and blunt honesty as he terms rudeness. A word might escape him, and the secret of Clarisse's birth become known. Yes, I must rid myself of him, then her feelings shall be mastered—suppressed. Discovery will ensue else,—her silence secured by persuading her that which now appears a crime, was merely an act of justice. A father's authority is my safe guard.

GALON *re-enters, jumping in a sack*, L.

Gal. We're all looking for you, sir; waiting in the garden to drink your health—long life to you—hurra!

La R. Thank you—amuse yourselves.

Gal. We do, bless you. Come and see us, it'll do your heart good; climbing up poles, jumping in sacks. I'll jump you for a wager.

[*Jumps and falls.* LA ROCHE *smiles and exits*, L.

Hallo! that won't do—we must start fair. *(jumps after him.)*

[*Shouts heard without*, L·

SCENE III.—*The gardens of Isle d'Amour occupying all the stage, the whole is profusely lit up with gas lamps. Trees in avenues, running up the stage*, R. *A decorated pavilion*, L. *An orchestra. At the back, a tavern seen through the trees— set orange trees. Statues, &c. When the scene opens, all the workmen and their wives are surrounding* LA ROCHE. *Shouting.*

Omnes. Long live the governor! *(shouts).*

Bobo. Huzza!

La R. Thank you, friends, thank you, enjoy yourselves.

Enter CLARISSE *leaning on* MADAME DONTEL'S *arm*, U. E. R. *pale and dejected.*

I perceive my daughter. We wish to be alone a few moments.

[*They all disperse over the gardens.* LA ROCHE *approaches* CLARISSE.

Cla. (*seeing him, shudders*). Ah! [*Involuntarily goes back.*

La R. You seem better?

Mad. D. Yes, and the fête will enliven her—nothing like dancing for the mopes.

Cla. Heavens! Alone with him! *(shudders).*

Mad. D, The girl weeps and tells me nothing, and the father bids me go, and this they call a confidential companion.

[*Exit up stage.* L·

La. R. Since yesterday, I have left you to yourself?

Cla. For which, I thank you. I wanted time to supplicate

heaven for strength and courage. I wanted tears to ease my aching heart.

La. R. It is indispensable that an explanation should take place between us respecting what you saw in ———

Cla. (placing her hand before her eyes.) Spare me that recollection. Let me blot out the memory of what I—I saw there. *(shudders).*

La R. (snatching her hand). Be mistress of yourself, they will notice your agitation.

Cla. Why—why did you oblige me to come here?

La R. Prudence! you must appear with your father calm and happy.

Cla. There is no more happiness for me—the knowledge of your guilt will kill me.

La R. It is of this I wish to speak—justify myself.

Cla. Justify mur— mur— *(checks herself, almost choking).* Do this—relieve my mind from this terrible weight that now oppresses it—prove your innocence, and I will worship you.— Innocence! Oh, no! no! I saw too plainly, crime! bloodshed!

La R. Girl!

Cla. I—I will be calm. Speak, I pray you! Prove what you say. It must be easy for an innocent father to prove his innocence to his child?

La R. (quickly, after watching round). The man, Martial, you introduced to me yesterday, was my bitter foe. He spoke insolently, menacing my name, reputation, and memory of your mother.

Cla. My mother! This is the first time I ever heard that name from your lips.

La R. He used threats—violence—a blow. I was compelled to defend my life. I had no time to reflect. Vengeance was in my grasp—he died. A word, or suspicious look from you, may bring me to the scaffold.

Cla. You are safe. I cannot accuse *you. (mournfully, aside).* Pardon him, heaven! Pardon his crime, in mercy to my mother's memory!

La R. No more tears or sadness. The remembrance of last night will soon pass away.

Cla. (aside). Never! never!

ROBERT *re-enters,* U. E. R. *with* ARMAND.

La R. I've been long expecting you.

Cla. (surprised). Armand!

La R. Yes, love, by my wish.

Rob. I was only just in time to bring him, he'd mounted the diligence to leave Paris.

La R. Why?

Arm. To raise the money stolen from you. My mother

possesses a small farm, it would have been sold to redeem the honour of her son.

La R. You're a good lad; think no more of it—return to your place.

Rob. I knew he'd do justice to him.

Arm. This is more than I expected, sir.

La R. Not more than you deserve. Now you may go to your mother if you like and ask her consent to your marriage.

Arm. With whom?

La R. Clarisse.

Cla. I—I—*(joyfully).* Are my senses deceiving me?

Rob. *(with great feeling).* How could I ever reproach you with unkindness, sir? You are better than a thousand fathers. I—I ask your pardon. *(wipes a tear aside).*

La R. *(to* CLARISSE*).* Are you happy?

Cla. *(with tears in her eyes).* How can I express my gratitude?

La R. *(aside).* I'll answer for her silence, now. You'll remain for the fête? *(to* ARMAND*).*

Arm. With your permission, I'd rather go home at once, unless Clarisse wishes it.

Cla. No, no, go!

La R. Perhaps you are right, it will only delay your wedding—embrace your wife and bid her farewell.

Arm. *(kissing* CLARISSE*)* Adieu! love.

Cla. Return speedily.

Arm. Never fear. Adieu!

> [*Shakes* ROBERT'S *hand.* ARMAND *leads off* CLARISSE,
> U. E. R. LA ROCHE *offers his hand, she shudders.*
> BARBILLON *and* MELANIE *enter the Gardens, he
> is dressed in a Tambour Major's coat and cocked
> hat. She very fine.*

Bar. *(bows conceitedly* R. *and* L. MELANIE *curtseying)* Hope we havn't kept you waiting, our carriage couldn't get up before.

Omnes. *(laughing)* Barbillon!

Bar. And Madame Barbillon, rather a fine specimen, eh? Something to look at, eh?

Mel. *(simpers)* Don't, I'am ashamed.

Rob. Where did you pick up that dress?

Bar. In the mud. Last night when I left your boat I found a poor devil floating under it.

La R *(starts)* Ah!

Bar. I dragged him ashore.

La R. *(agitated)* Dead?

Bar. As a herring. The Humane Society paid me 15 francs, and I bought this suit, its the last new fashion.

La R. All is secure. Enjoy yourselves, friends.

Omnes. We will! we will!

Mel. I never saw such a fine place—such heaps of sugar plums, and heavenly excitement. Order wine and crack me some nuts.

Bar. Who's to pay? I don't mind a little sugar and water.

Mel. I'm hungry.

Bar. Dancing will take away your appetite—where's the orchestra?

Gal. Here. (*strikes guitar down* L.)

Omnes. Music! music! *(Musicians in the orchestra).*

Bar. Take your places, turn out your toes, cock up your noses, turn and twist in and out, up and down, and blaze away.

Gal. No, no, we'll have the polka first, Barbillon—Canal Polka—hurrah for St. Martin's.

Omnes. No! no! a song.

SONG—GALON.

Who so happy as we, boys,
Life for us gives all her joys—
And, to my poor thinking,
Its joys are all in drinking,
For good wine's a jolly soul.
Fill, fill up your glasses,
Toast and kiss the lasses,
Hip, hip, huzza—hip, hip, huzza,
Bumpers lads—blaze away.

The miser he lives crying—
The lover fondly sighing—
A fig for all their dying,
Good drink there's no denying
Is a hearty jolly soul.

Fill, fill up, &c.

Sweet beauty fond caressing,
Their cherry lips now pressing,
Transports fill the soul;
Yet all these joys confessing,
Still give me the rosy bowl.

Fill, fill up, &c.

[*At end of song, omnes shout.* A speech, a speech.

Bar. (bowing) Ladies and gents—for the honour you've done me I—I—

Omnes. Hear, hear!

Bar. This—the proudest moment—life—hem—ever engraved here. *(touches his heart.)* Allow me to—to return sincere—hem—grateful thanks hoping—hem—wishing—hem —you may—may get the rest. [*All laugh.*

Omnes. Come a dance, the Polka, the dance.

> [*Polka danced by* MELANIE *and* BARBILLON, *at the end, all the workmen and their wives dance with great animation and laughter. The men beat time with keys on bottles during the song.*

La R. Bravo! bravo!

> MARTIAL *entering* U. E. *elegantly dressed.*

Mar. Bravo! charming! *(comes* L.*)*
La R. (*astonished*) Living!
Cla. (*aside*) Thank Heaven!
Bar. Is it you? The man I pulled out—
Mar. And saved from drowning—a wretch threw me into the water. I trust this will excuse my arriving so late, my dear friend.
La R. We—we—we are—
Mar. Enchanted to see me—I anticipate your good feeling

> [*To* MARTIAL.

Bar. You owe me ten francs—my diving prices are for gentlemen twenty-five francs, workmen ten, children five, women nothing—I always let them sink.
Mar. There are twenty, my good fellow.
Bar. Huzza! we'll spend it all. Come, Melanie, come,—wine, nuts.

> [*Music.—All exeunt with* BARBILLON R. *and* L. *at every wing, singing,* "La-la-la." BARBILLON *dances with* MELANIE.

Mar. What a deep dog you are. (*to* LA ROCHE.)
La R. (*to* CLARISSE) Join Madame Dontel. (CLARISSE *retires up.*) If you wish to sacrifice me, do so, at once.
Mar. Certainly not—you are too valuable at present. On one condition I am silent.
La R. Name it.
Mar. Two hundred thousand francs, and the hand of Clarisse.
La R. Your wife! Never.
Mar. Yes, and you'll be my dear papa, if not the scaffold—reflect.

> [*Joins some Ladies in conversation.*

Cla. (*watching anxiously, and rejoining her father* R.) I cannot rest until assured of your safety. Will he denounce you?
La R. All's well.

> JOHN *heard crying without, and* ROBERT *re-enters* U. E. R. *dragging him forward.*

John. Let me go—let me go.

Rob. Not till this affair's cleared up ; your master must explain it before all present.

> [A COMMISSARY OF POLICE *and four police enter*
> *rapidly* U. E. R , *workmen, guests assemble*
> *round.*

La R. Police! may I be allowed to enquire the motive of your visit here, sir ?

Com. (to MARTIAL*)* You stated this morning that you knew the author of your attempted assassination.

Cla. Lost! (*with deep emotion.*)

Com. On visiting your house, I found this person only ; (*pointing to* JOHN) questioning him, I found he had heard the name of the criminal.

Cla. I am dying.

Mar. Babbling idiot !

Com. We are determined to ascertain the truth and bring the villain to justice.

La R. (to MARTIAL*)* Save me and I consent to all. (*quickly*).

Mar. The money and her hand ?

La R. All, all.

Mar. I would rather forgive—forget—than venture to make such a heavy accusation.

Com. You can't evade it.   Your servant already accuses —

Rob. Me ! The rascal !   That's what I want cleared up.

John Didn't he threaten your life yesterday?   And last night I saw him steal from the boat at ten.

Bar. (R.) At a quarter past, I fished you up. (*to* MARTIAL).   But I'm sure Robert's innocent.

Omnes. O, yes ! yes !

Mar. (aside). A brilliant idea !

Com. What do you say, sir.

Mar. That he is guilty, I cannot deny it.

Rob. I—I— (*the* POLICE *secure him*).

Cla. (running to LA ROCHE*).* You will not let them accuse an innocent man—see him dragged to prison—suffer disgrace —death for this horrid lie ?

La R. (low and aside). Your   promise—a word, and I perish.

Com. (to CLARISSE*).* Madame Clarisse you appear to know—

Cla. N— n— nothing !

> [*Faltering, then stands statue-like, perfectly absorbed.*
> ROBERT *is slowly removed.* MARTIAL *takes*
> LA ROCHE's *hand.* BARBILLON *weeps; all are*
> *affected. Music*

END OF ACT II.

ACT III.

SCENE I.—*A Room in* La Roche's *house, in the flat a window* L. *A door* S. E. L. *Door,* F. R. MUSIC. CLARISSE *discovered at the window in flat, she appears to be watching anxiously.*

Cla. (sighing) No one comes   I relied on that young man, thinking him attached to poor Robert. He promised to let me hear often of—of the prisoner, but has deceived me. For three days I've watched constantly, anxiously for his arrival ; he believes him guilty, like all the world, and leaves him to his wretched fate. Who—who has reduced him to this?—my father ! *(shudders.)* Conscience-stricken, he avoids me since Robert was arrested, shutting himself up for days together from every one but Monsieur Martial, that man whose looks and words are loathsome to me ! Must the innocent perish for the crimes of the guilty ? Merciful Providence forbid it.

Mel. (pops her head in window from flat) May I come in.

Cla. Who are you ?

Mel. A friend of Barbillon's, he has sent me to you.

Cla. (runs to window) Has he seen Robert ?

MELANIE *enters,* D. F.

Mel. Yes, Ma'amselle, he swam into the prison up one of the water spouts.

Cla. Do they believe him guilty ? will they condemn him ? Can they ?

Mel. Barbillon has some doubts, and, to prevent accidents, means to take him up the spout, it leads to a subterranean passage outside the prison walls.

Cla. Now I comprehend you.

Mel When Barbillon proposed it to Robert, first he hesitated, saying, " I have been accused wrongfully, but if I fly, escape thus, Ma'amselle Clarisse will think me guilty—I'd rather remain and brave the worst."

Cla. He told him what I had said, did he not ? that I would pledge my life on his innocence.

Mel. Of course he did ; then the old gentleman jumped up and frisked about for joy like a fly in a mustard-pot, and consented as the clock strikes nine to go up the spout, I am going to watch their coming down.

Cla. Lose not an instant, my good girl.

Mel. If all is right Barbillon will be under this window by nine. If he's not here——

Cla. What then?

Mel. He'll be somewhere else too difficult to guess, poor fellow. But never fear, Ma'amselle, Heaven is just, and Barbillon climbs like a cat, its beautifully grand to see him mount a greasy pole and gracefully snatch the prize, a leg of mutton or an infant pig! Such dignity! Oh ye Gods! why wasn't I a man and a climber. [*Exit.* D. F.

Cla. There is a ray of hope, though slight and fragile its foundation, all my hopes of happiness are anchored there.

LA ROCHE *enters passively and silent from door* L.

La R. Clarisse, grave matters render it necessary for us to talk together, instantly.

Cla. Is it concerning Robert? I know it is not in your power to liberate him by denying the charge brought against him; you would be happy if he left France for ever, would you not, dear father?

La R. Explain yourself.

Cla. In his misfortunes he has found friends, he will be free, liberated from prison to-night.

La R. Free! and I shall be condemned.

Cla. Who will betray you?

La R. Martial! Unless I fulfil his conditions.

Cla. If he demand money give it him.

La R. That is not all—he seeks your hand.

Cla. Mine! I his wife! Oh! no—no.

La R. His silence can only be purchased at that price.

Cla. And will you consent to this? Has he not outraged the memory of my mother? Is he not a slanderous perjurer? Can you sacrifice me to him knowing my heart is another's?

La R. Knowing this I ask nothing, but am resigned to my doom——we see each other for the last time.

Cla. Is there no other way to enforce his silence?

La R. None—your hand or a felon's death. Let it be so; better I suffer than your feelings be outraged.

Cla. Don't talk thus—give me time to reflect—a day or two—my brain wanders. (*presses her head.*) Armand.

La R. Whatever is done must be to-day.

Cla. To-day! Armand—I—

La R. The contract must be signed at nine.

Cla. (*aside, with great feeling*) Heaven! you who have heard my prayers, dictate the line of conduct I ought to pursue, enable me to fulfil my task, I beseech. My father's life, the author of my being, on the one side—my affections, hopes, happiness, on the other. The struggle's too fearful, support me I pray. (*crosses to* L.)

La R. The fatal hour is nigh—it is not fit you should witness my arrest—leave me.

Cla (*firmly*) I shall remain.   To-night, before the signing of this contract, I shall know if Robert's saved or lost—if lost, ask nothing of me—I could not, to save the world, give my hand to the man whose perjury had brought an innocent creature to the scaffold.

La R. (*quickly*) If he is saved—

Cla. (*trembling*). I consent to what this man requires.

Mar. (*without* L.) M. La Roche is waiting for me.

Cla. His voice!   Let me go!

La R. Will you not let him learn his happiness from *your* lips ?

Cla. (*laughing bitterly*). Happiness!   You talk to me of happiness !   Oh ! father, father, where is your heart ?

[*Bursts into tears, and exit* R.

La R. After all, my life is to depend on Robert's, eh ! Agreeable !   I'll dissemble—dictate to me—poor fools—my terms with all shall be death.

Enter MARTIAL, L.

Mar. Well, what success ?   Does your lovely daughter consent ?   Are you to be my respected papa?

La R. I am going to fetch the notary to draw up the contract.   Remember your promise, (*cross to* L.) if the marriage take place ?

Mar. And the money's touched,—I say, good bye for ever; the word of a gentleman's sufficient.

La R. Agreed. (*aside*). Any thing to escape his infernal influence.　　　　　　　　　　　　　　　　[*Exit* L.

Mar. Adieu, adieu, dear papa.   All goes gloriously.   Once rich, blessed with beauty, I'm off.   My departure's already prepared.   If my respectable companion's suspected.   A few objections might be raised; as they know nothing, it wouldn't be polite to disturb their feelings.

Enter MADAME DONTEL, L.

Mad. D. Your servant, sir; wish you joy.   There is a person wishes to see you on business of importance, he wont take a denial.

Enter JOHN *disguised, with a large nose and very stout,* L.

John. (*in an assumed voice*). I wants Mynheer?

[MADAME DONTEL *exits.* R

Mar. Who are you ?

John. I am Mynheer Deidrick Slishervisherknockunderhausen.

Mar. A very pretty name.

John. I heard from old Frow, you wanted a servant ?

Mar. I require none. No more foreigners; I had quite enough of master John, he robbed me.

John. (in his natural voice). Devil a bit.

Mar. (starting). John—

John. Cabot. We haven't seen you these eight days, and began to be fearful of your health, so I disguised myself to look after you.

Mar. You are all fools; I am settling affairs.

John. That's it, we want to settle 'em with you.

Mar. You fear to trust me?

John. Not at all—only we'd rather not. We must share the money La Roche is to pay, if not, we'll spoil your sport.

Mar. Well—to night.

John. The old place? Round roads?

Mar. Yes, yes—begone. Madame Dontel returns.

MADAME DONTEL *re-enters,* L.

Mad. D. The notary is here, sir?

Mar. (to JOHN). My good friend, I require no servant.

Mad. D. (aside). What an animal for service.

John. (going). Oh mi, Ladi. *(aside).* He's going to give us the slip, I fancy. Will he? *(shakes his head).* Oh, no! [*Exit* L.

Mad D. I'll call Ma'mselle. [*Exit* R.

LA ROCHE *and* NOTARY *enter,* L.

La R. Be seated, sir. (NOTARY *sits*). Fill up these blanks, sir. *(points to contract).*

CLARISSE *enters with* MADAME DONTEL, R., *her eyes cast down*

La R. (aside to her). Remember, my life is in your hands?.

Cla. I cannot forget, sir.

La R. (looks over the NOTARY). I give two hundred thousand francs after the ceremony.

Mar. Before, if you please, papa?

La R. Before!

[NOTARY *writes.* LAROCHE *never leaves* CLARISSE.

Not. All is ready. [*Presents pen to* CLARISSE.

La R. My child. *(nine o'clock strikes).* Come, come.

Cla. (listening) Nine! *(she runs to window and throws it up.)*

Mar. What is all this. *(to* LA ROCHE.) Pierre Bernard, take care—no tricks.

Bar. (heard singing without.) "The Bird is free."

Cla. Preserved! saved! *(clasps her hands and runs to the table.)* Now, now, I sign—father, quickly, quickly.

[*Signs contract, then mildly sinks on a chair.* MA-DAME DONTEL *runs to her.*

Mar. (signs) The money's mine!

John. (*peeping in at window in flat*) Halves, governor.
Cla. You are saved !

> [*Music.   Scene closes on picture.*

SCENE II.—*Le Chemin de Ronde.   A desolate gloomy pile of buildings, abutting on a road unfinished.   Stage dark.   Music.*

> PIPOD *and* LOUCHON *steal on separately.* R. & L.

Pip. (L.) Who goes there ?
Lou. (R.) Birds of the night.
Pip. Louchon.   Where's John Cabot ?
John. (*creeping on* L.) Here.   Don't bawl so, Martial's coming.
Pip. Are you certain ?
John. As he won't come to us, we'll go to him—his wedding. (*Voices heard in the distance.*) Make yourselves scarce.

> [*Military music.   They conceal themselves.   A patrol enters* F. E. R., *cross stage and exeunt* F. E. L., BARBILLON *follows them* F. E. R.

Bar. This way, I know the road. (*beckons on* ROBERT, *he enters slowly* F. E. R.)   We'll leave Paris with the market people, once past the barriers, huzza for Flanders !   Orders have been given by La Roche for a swift boat, you'll soon be sailing away from France—never to return.
Rob. Its useless, I can't go.
Bar. Not go !   after all the trouble I've taken.
Rob. No.   I'd rather return to prison than quit France without seeing Clarisse.
Bar. What an obstinate perverse old chap you are—you'll spoil her wedding day.
Rob. Clarisse going to marry ?
Bar. So Madame Dontel told me.
Rob. I'm glad of it, Armand will make her happy, they love each other truly.   I'll give them my blessing—see them before I bid my native land good night.
Bar. Good night—I should like to bid it good morning.
Rob. Ah !   you cannot enter into my feelings.   Ask the mendicant who starves on his hard-wrung pittance, why he does not leave ?
Bar. Why !   because he's a fool.
Rob. Ask the felon who weeps when the ship which is to bear him into exile is under weigh, why he weeps ?—Ask the soldier fighting his country's battles in foreign lands why he dreals of home ?   Why does the mariner rejoice when he leaps on his native shore ?   Because it is our only home, all else is exile.   [*Exit* R.
Bar. Oh !   he's cracked—not used to the spout (*follows him cautiously.*)   Poor fellow   [*The gang watch them off.*
John. How did he escape from prison ?

MARTIAL *enters* s. E. R. *disguised in a blouse, cap, &c., the gang crouch on the ground.*

Mar. This is the rendezvous for the last time, to-morrow I bid my friends—

John Pip. & Lou. (surround him)—Welcome.

Mar. Delighted to see you, gentlemen. What is your pleasure with me?

John. Business—the two hundred thousand francs.

Mar. My wife's portion? I can't touch it.

John. We can and will.

Mar. Not a franc.

John. Then into the canal you go, with a stone round your neck—no floating this time. [*They seize him.*

Mar. This is rude, gentlemen.

John. Will you divide the money with us?

Mars. Yes, I give you my honour.

John. I should like something better. Suppose we honour your marriage with our company?

Omnes. Yes!

Mar. With all my heart, I invite you. *(aside).* I'll have 'em all seized.

John. That's jolly—a rare day, eh, lads? Feasting, dancing, money.

Mar. You dont forget that?

John. Rather not. But you won't appear as bridegroom in that dress?

Mar. I'm well provided.

> [*Throws off blouse, cap, and high over-alls, draws flat hat from his pocket, and pulls off his rabbit skin gloves, he is then attired elegantly, kid gloves, glazed boots, &c.*

John. So are we.

> [*They all throw off their disguises, and are dressed as fashionables.*

If you had not invited us, we should have been there.

Mar. Cunning dogs! there's no doing you. Your hand's, boys, we'll share all fairly. I admire your wit.

Omnes. Huzza! [*They shake hands.*

Mar. Mind, Pipod and Louchon, are college friends?

John. I'm your rich old uncle, come to give you away. *(laughs).* What a give! Oh! oh! [*All laugh.*

Mar. We beakfast at ten, gentlemen?

John. We'll be there at nine.

Mar. (bowing low). I have the honour.

Omnes. We all have the honour.

Mar. Adieu!

> [*Shakes hands and backs, all shaking their hands and backing out opposite.*

SCENE LAST.—*Fête of the Barrier St. Martin, whole stage occupied with stalls, swings, decorated poles. Canal with boats. Quays, L. Exterior of* LA ROCHE's *house, with grated gate. When the scene opens, the stage is filled with persons, male and female, enjoying the fête, laughing and singing, climbing, swinging. Lemondiers, Workmen, Soldiers, Grisettes, Students, Bourgeoise.* MELANIE *gaily dressed, pushes through the crowd, loaded with toys and flowers.*

Mel. Pretty treatment !   This Barbillon has left me to carry all my souvenirs and bon bons, while he looks after that Monsieur Robert.   Leaves me to the mercy of the mob on a fête day.   What'll he do after the fatal knot's tied. (*sighs*). He bought me a *ginger bread man*, as a token of love, and told me to amuse myself. (*shows ginger bread figure*). Nice amusement in this. (*bites the head off*). How very hot his love is, all ginger and pepper. (*a man touches her back with a rattle and runs off.   She starts*). If you dare do that again, (*as she turns to remonstrate, another person does the same, laughs and runs off,*) I'll tear your eyes out. I shall be scratched to death. (*cries, then calls*). Barbillon, you little viper !   He calls this giving one a treat.   I want to go home.   No, I wont !   I'll stay and spend all his money in snapdragon and nonsense.

> [*Another person touches her with rattle.   Enraged,*
> *she throws all the toys at him.   Crowd laugh.*
> *She runs up the stage, calling* Police ! Guard !

BARBILLON *entering from* LA ROCHE's *house,* L.

Bar. Now, I think the thing's all arranged comfortably, while the visitors and bridal party are engaged eating and drinking with La Roche.   Ma'amselle Clarisse will slip into the garden to speak with Robert and bid him good bye.   I have begged her not to tell the poor old man anything about her marriage with Monsieur Martial, as he fancies it is with Monsieur Armand.   To open his eyes, would drive him wild; he'd never leave France then, and all my trouble be wasted. I've got him snug on board the boat—no one suspects.   The interview over, he starts for Flanders, and I start for matrimony with Melanie.

Mel. (re-entering). No you dont, sir !   Paltry fellow, to leave me with a ginger bread man !   There's a ginger bread woman to keep him company, that's too good for you.

> [*Throws it at him and goes up.*

Bar. My love, my dear, what have I done ?
Mel. Nothing but plague me.
Bar. I've spent all my money ?
Mel. Yes, but you borrowed it first; I lent it to you.
Bar. Hush ! I'll repay it by-and-bye. Let's get Robert away, out of the reach of his enemies, and I'll never leave you again.

Mel. You wont, upon your word? And shall I have a swing and a round-about?

Bar. Every thing when we are married, sweet!

Mel. Oh, I want to be married?

Bar. Stop! stop! You must lend me the tin to buy the ring.

Mel. I can't; you spent it all in chickweed.

Bar. I'm a shareholder in the canal mud, and will sell out to sport the dust.

> [*Exits up stage with* MELANIE. *As they go up,* AR-
> MAND, *in a travelling dress, enters, carrying a
> small portmanteau.*

Arm. (looking at LA ROCHE'S *house).* I can't account for the strange presentiment that agitates me; it has pressed on my spirits during the whole of my journey. I find the inner yard closed—no work. *(approaches gate).* What a number of people in the gardens, all gaily dressed. What can it mean? I wish I could see Robert, and learn before I ring.

> [*Enter* BARBILLON *conducting* ROBERT, U. R. R. *His
> hat slouched over his eyes and collar of his coat up.*

Bar. Push your hat over your eyes and pull up your collar, you'll never be known then.

Arm. Barbillon! Robert!

Rob. Armand!

Bar. (aside). The fat's in the fire now.

Arm. (shaking ROBERT'S *hand).* I'm delighted to see you.

Rob. So am I—I couldn't go without saying farewell and shaking your hand. Such a day as this—but how is it you're not dressed in your best?

Arm. I've only just quitted the Diligence?

Bar. Come, Robert, come. *(pulling him).*

Rob. Only just left the diligence?

Arm. No; I am here earlier than I expected—everything favors me, my mother consents. I long to see Clarisse.

Rob. Very natural, boy. Everything's prepared for your return.

Arm. I don't understand what all these people are doing in the garden.

Rob. Why you wouldn't marry alone, would you? They are the guests invited to your wedding.

Arm. Mine! You deceive yourself. I've only just arrived from Burgoyne.

Rob. (to BARBILLON.) What did you tell me?

Bar. It was only my fun.

Rob. You told me Clarisse was going to be married this morning.

Arm. Impossible.

Bar. So she is, but not to him. *(points to* ARMAND.)

Rob. If not with him, who is it? Speak, or I'll strangle you. (*violently seizing him.*)

Bar. If you will know you must—its to—

> [*Bells ring. The gates are opened and the bridal party enter from house.* GALON, MARTIN, *and Workmen and wives, all in gay attire.* MAD. DONTEL, JOHN, PIPOD, LOUCHON, MARTIAL, LAROCHE, CLARISSE, *in bridal costume.*

Bar (*points to* MARTIAL). That's the bridegroom, and I wish him joy.

Cla. Clarisse false!

Rob. No. There's fraud, trickery, in this, I won't suffer it. (BARBILLON *holds his coat.*)

Bar. Don't be foolish, you'll be discovered and sent back to prison.   [ROBERT *struggles.*

Mar. (*to* CLARISSE) Come, love.

Rob. (*rushing forward*) I bid her stay.

Omnes. Robert (*astonished*).

La R. What are you doing here, Robert? Pray retire, remember the danger you're exposed to.

Rob. I care for no danger, let them drag me back to my dungeon, but this marriage shall not take place.

Mar. That's cool.

La R. (*to* ROBERT). Think of your promise.

Rob. I think of nothing now, you have deceived three of us, the boy, Clarisse, myself.

Bar. He'd deceive the devil.

Rob. You seek to force the poor thing to marry this man— he that accused me—its infamous.

La R. (*aside*). If he speaks I am discovered.

Mar. Call the police, let the fellow be locked up. Now, friends, don't disturb yourselves. Ma'amselle the ceremony waits. (*to* CLARISSE, *offering his hand.*)

Rob. Let it wait! miserable wretch if you dare to lay a finger on her, I'll fell you to the earth, like a dog, as you are. I forbid this mockery of marriage.

Mar. (*sneers*) You! You are—

Rob. Her father.   [*All astounded.* JOHN *steals off.* F.E. L.

Cla. Father. (*runs to him.*)

Rob Yes, Clarisse, your father who has kept the secret through suffering and misery for twenty long years, to ensure your happiness—to save you from disgrace—your father who now claims his right at the peril of his life. Your true loving father, that comes to snatch you from infamy. (*embraces her.*) Tremble no more, my own sweet child, you are secure—I am here to save, protect you!

Mar. Not your own child, after all—you are a deep dog, papa.

JOHN *re-enters with* COMMISSARY OF POLICE, F. E. L. *points to* ROBERT.

Com. I arrest you as an escaped criminal. (*to* ROBERT, *police surround him.*)

Cla. You shall not take him from me—he is *my* father. I can speak now, proclaim his innocence of the crime you charge him with. I saw it committed, was in the boat when the assassin—(*looks at* LA ROCHE)—no, I cannot betray him. Speak, sir, say my father is not guilty.

La R. (*moved*) I—I do—I do—Robert is innocent.

Com. The proofs

La R. Are in my desk. Follow me.

[*Exit into house with* COMMISSARY S. E. L

Mar. He means—

John. Mischief. We'd better bid the lovely bride adieu.

Mar. Hush!

[*Report of a pistol within,* COMMISSARY *re-enters.*

Com. La Roche has confessed his guilt, and done justice on himself—he is dead. [CLARISSE *appears affected.*

Mar. Dead! Dear me! poor papa! (*aside*). The money's lost. I regret these unpleasant circumstances, and say, adieu!

[*Bows.*

John. We all say the same.

[PIPOD, LOUCHON *all bow.* COMMISSARY *points to* POLICE, *they secure them.*

John. Dont, I've done nothing—we are—

Com. A desperate gang of plunderers.

John. (*crying*) Who betrayed us?

Com. Martial!

John. ⎫
Pip. ⎬ Oh! the ———
Lou. ⎭

Mar. Extremely sorry, but justice — (*going,* POLICE *arrest him*).

Com. You are also our prisoner, as their leader!

Mar. I—I. Who gave me up?

John. (*laughing*). I did—extremely sorry—but justice!

Mar. Snared—(*smiles*)—fairly snared.

[*Mob laugh and point at them.*

Mar. (*bows to mob*). Really it's quite delightful to see so much good humour prevailing. (*to* OFFICER). Before I tear myself from those I love, allow me to speak. (*to* ARMAND). first, to the happy bridegroom, it is usual to wish joy. In the language of my English groom, I wish he may get it, for the fair bride even her beauty, I regret to think, must fade. Age will creep on, and I fondly trust that she may live long enough for her husband to think her old and ugly. Robert, my honest fellow, it pains me to part with you—farewell—live, live with your sweet children long enough to make them wish you, as I do, at the devil.   [*Bows and exit.*

Bar. Huzza! All the foxes have lost their tails in their own traps. Ah! Ha! ha!

Rob. (joining ARMAND *and* CLARISSE'S *hands).* You deserve her,—she is worthy of you. My children, be happy.

Cla. (pressing his hand). We are so—we are supremely so, dear father! Gratitude and joy for your preservation.—My escape—fill our hearts. Blest with your love, we have nothing to desire now—yes, yes. *(curtseys to audience).* Pardon.—Our felicity made me selfish, forgetful, for the moment, of those friends whose smiles ever welcome our efforts, without your approbation, there is no happiness for Clarisse.

THE END.

Disposition of Characters.

R.   L.

ALL THE VILLAGERS AND CHORUS.

MADAME DONTEL, ROBERT, CLARISSE, ARMAND, MELANIE, BARBILLON.

W. S. Johnson, "Nassau Steam Press," 60, St. Martin's Lane.

SPLENDID NEW EDITION OF PLAYS.

WEBSTER'S
ACTING NATIONAL DRAMA,

UNDER THE AUSPICES OF THE DRAMATIC AUTHORS' SOCIETY.

This Edition comprises every successful New Play, Farce, Melo-Drama, &c. produced at the London Theatres, **correctly** printed from the Prompter's Copy.

A NUMBER WILL BE PUBLISHED EVERY FORTNIGHT, PRICE SIXPENCE.

(THE MORE EXPENSIVE COPYRIGHTS ONE SHILLING.)

Each Play will be illustrated by an Etching of the most interesting Scene taken during the representation, by PIERCE EGAN THE YOUNGER.

VOLUME I.

With a Portrait of J. R. PLANCHE, F.S.A., price 7s. in cloth, contains :—

VOLUME II.

With a Portrait of TYRONE POWER, Esq., price 7s. cloth, contains :—

VOLUME III.

With a Portrait of C. MATHEWS, Esq. price 7s. cloth, contains :—

VOLUME IV.

With a Portrait of T. HAYNES BAYLY, Esq., price 7s. cloth, contains

WEBSTER'S ACTING NATIONAL DRAMA.
PRICE SIXPENCE.

VOLUME V.
With a Portrait of J. B. BUCKSTONE, Esq., price 7s. cloth, contains:—

51. WHITE HORSE OF THE PEPPERS
52. GEMINI.
53. THE ARTIST'S WIFE.
54. A LESSON FOR LADIES
55. THE DEVIL'S OPERA
56. TOM NODDY'S SECRET
57. FORTY AND FIFTY.
58. SONS AND SYSTEMS.
59. PRINTER'S DEVIL.
60. ASK NO QUESTIONS.
61. "BUT HOWEVER—"
62. NICHOLAS NICKLEBY.
63. MARRIED LIFE.

VOLUME VI.
With a Portrait of B. WEBSTER, Esq., price 7s. cloth, contains:—

64. OLIVER TWIST.
65. CHAOS IS COME AGAIN.
66. MR. GREENFINCH.
67. MY LITTLE ADOPTED.
68. MAID OF CROISSEY.
69. GRACE DARLING.
70. THE COURT OF OLD FRITZ.
71. JANE LOMAX.
72. "QUEEN'S HORSE."
73. BURLINGTON ARCADE.
74. HIS FIRST CHAMPAGNE.
75. IZAAK WALTON.
76. SWISS SWAINS.

VOLUME VII.
With a Portrait of BAYLE BERNARD, Esq., price 7s. cloth, contains:—

77. SAYINGS AND DOINGS.
78. DR. DILWORTH.
79. THE HAPPY MAN.
80. SCHOOL FOR SCANDAL, 1s.
81. SINGLE LIFE, 1s.
82. THE VILLAGE DOCTOR.
83. THE HALL PORTER.
84. KING O'NEIL.
85. JACK SHEPPARD, 1s.
86. HIS LAST LEGS.

VOLUME VIII.
With a Portrait of J. S. KNOWLES, Esq., price 7s. cloth, contains:—

87. THE DREAM AT SEA, 1s.
88. H.B.
89. VICTORINE, 1s.   [1s.
90. HENRIETTE THE FORSAKEN,
91. THE WRECK ASHORE, 1s.
92. ISABELLE, 1s.
93. BRIAN BOROIHME, 1s.
(Written by Sheridan Knowles, Esq.)

VOLUME IX.
94. THE FORTUNES OF SMIKE.
95. HOBBS, DOBBS, & STUBBS.
96. THE IRISH ATTORNEY.
97. HOW TO PAY THE RENT.
98. THE PLACE HUNTER.
99. THE GREEK BOY.
100. BOARDING SCHOOL, 1s.
101. THE WOMAN HATER.
102. A LOVER BY PROXY.
103. PETER & PAUL, 1s.
104. LOCOMOTION.

VOLUME X.
105. ALMA MATER. 1s.
106. GRANDFATHER WHITEHEAD
107. CURIOSITIES OF LITERATURE
108. THE LAST DAY.
109. WHO'S YOUR FRIEND?
110. CAUGHT IN A TRAP. 1s.
111. THE THIMBLE RIG.
112. THE FOX AND THE GOOSE.
113. CÆSAR DE BAZAN.   [1s.
114. THE MYSTERIOUS STRANGER,

VOLUME XI.
115. THE CHIMES, 1s.
116. THE GREEN BUSHES; OR, A HUNDRED YEARS AGO, 1s.
117. THE MOTHER AND CHILD ARE DOING WELL.
118. THE SHERIFF OF THE COUNTY. [1s.
119. ST. GEORGE & THE DRAGON.
120. THE IRISH DRAGOON. .
121. CLARISSE.   [1s

Also, demy 8vo., QUID PRO QUO; OR, THE DAY OF DUPES, and OLD HEADS AND YOUNG HEARTS.—Price 2s. 6d. each.

SPLENDID PORTRAITS. PRICE 1s. EACH.
J. R. PLANCHE, Esq.—The late TYRONE POWER, Esq.—CHARLES MATHEWS, Esq.—The late THOMAS HAYNES BAYLY, Esq.—J. B. BUCKSTONE, Esq.—BENJAMIN WEBSTER, Esq.—JAMES SHERIDAN KNOWLES, Esq.

W. S. JOHNSON, "NASSAU STEAM PRESS," 60, ST. MARTIN'S LANE.